Greetings from San Diego

U.S. NAVAL HOSPITAL CHAPEL, SAN DIEGO, CALIF.—18

Mme. Schumann Heink,
near San Diego. Cal.

Schiffer Publishing Ltd ®

4880 Lower Valley Road, Atglen, PA 19310 USA

Mary L. Martin,
Tina Skinner, and
Lindsey Hamilton

3804 Birds'-eye View Looking West from Timpkin Building, San Diego, California

Designed by Mark David Bowyer
Type set in ZapfChancery MdIt BT / Korinna BT

ISBN: 0-7643-2562-0
Printed in China

Published by Schiffer Publishing Ltd.
4880 Lower Valley Road
Atglen, PA 19310
Phone: (610) 593-1777; Fax: (610) 593-2002
E-mail: Info@schifferbooks.com

For the largest selection of fine reference books on this and related subjects, please visit our web site at
www.schifferbooks.com
We are always looking for people to write books on new and related subjects. If you have an idea for a book please contact us at the above address.

This book may be purchased from the publisher.
Include $3.95 for shipping.
Please try your bookstore first.
You may write for a free catalog.

In Europe, Schiffer books are distributed by
Bushwood Books
6 Marksbury Ave.
Kew Gardens
Surrey TW9 4JF England
Phone: 44 (0) 20 8392-8585; Fax: 44 (0) 20 8392-9876
E-mail: info@bushwoodbooks.co.uk
Website: www.bushwoodbooks.co.uk
Free postage in the U.K., Europe; air mail at cost.

Contents

Introduction

The San Diego area was home to Native Americans for thousands of years before its discovery by Juan Rodriguez Cabrillo in 1542. Sixty years later, another Spanish explorer, Sebastian Viscaino, came to the land and named it San Diego, after Saint Didacus of Alcala. San Diego was claimed by Spain, although settlement did not begin until 1768. In April 1769, a group of Franciscan Friars came to shore and began to establish the California missions.

The beautiful beaches, warm weather, and luscious landscape enticed settlers. They came seeking health, wealth, and a better lifestyle. With the help of several wealthy investors and determined citizens, San Diego rose to greatness. From the fictional romance novel that ignited a nationwide love affair with California to the Panama-California Exposition in 1915—which celebrated the newly created shortcut between East and West—San Diego has been an object of lifestyle lust for almost two centuries.

Critical military bases have played a key role in the economic growth of this westernmost city. The Navy first established its presence here in 1907, and since then San Diego has become home to Marine Corp., U.S. Navy, and Coast Guard operations. San Diego claims to be the birthplace of Naval aviation, and its skies are never without planes, both military and commercial.

The postcard images in this book give readers a chance to watch the city grow and develop, embrace its heritage, and become the seventh largest city in the United States; they record the growth and spirit of San Diego. Cards going to every corner of the country speak about the wonderful weather, the beautiful buildings, and the laid back lifestyle of the city. People stuck on the crowded and chilly East Coast were often taunted with descriptions of beaches and open space. As one card reads, "I'll pick an orange for you, and you can throw a snowball for me." The messages on the postcards often vocalize the senders' thoughts of the city and their experience. "I'm having a great time," or "The ocean is beautiful" reinforce the visual message of the card itself. Long before e-mail, postcards allowed travelers and those who had moved away from family and friends to reach out over thousands of miles and share their joy and experiences. Luckily, they've been preserved and recreated in this beautiful collection.

Ruins of Mission San Diego de Alcala.

Circa 1910, $3-5

S. D. 1   MAP OF SAN DIEGO BAY, CALIFORNIA

This overview of San Diego highlights the area communities in 1910. The greater area includes La Jolla on the far right, Point Loma at the mouth of the bay, and Coronado Heights on the far left.

Copyright 1910, $6-8

San Diego homes and bay.

Copyright 1910, $7-9

El Cabrillo National Monument commemorates the discovery of the state of California. From the back: "Here at Point Loma Head on September 28, 1542, Juan Rodriguez Cabrillo, distinguished Portuguese Navigator in the service of Spain, made his first landing, thus discovering what is now the State of California."

Circa 1950s, $2-4

Spectators enjoy an orchestral show at The Ford Bowl in Balboa Park. The U.S. Naval Hospital is in the background.

Circa 1940, $4-6

In a time of more relaxed border security, a monument is pictured in nearby Tijuana, marking the international boundary between the United States and Mexico.

Circa 1910, $3-5

4626. Watching the Bathers, La Jolla,
San Diego, Calif.

Bathers and onlookers gather on the beach at La Jolla.

Cancelled 1924, $7-9

About Historic Postcard Images

Postcards are said to be the most popular collectible history has ever known. The urge to horde them sprang up with the birth of this means of communication at the turn of the 20th century, and has endured great changes in the printing industry. Today, postcard shows take place every weekend somewhere in the country, or the world, and millions of pieces of ephemera lie in wait for those who collect obscure topics or town views.

Postcards once served as the e-mail of their day. They were the fastest, most popular means of communication beginning in the 1890s in the United States. These timely cards provided a way to send visual scenes through the mail along with brief messages—a way to enchant friends and family with the places travelers visited, to send local scenes, or to share favorite topics of imagery. They even provided the latest breaking news, as images of fires, floods, shipwrecks, and festivals were often available in postcard form within hours of an event. Moreover, mail was delivered to most urban homes in the United States at least twice a day. So someone might send a morning postcard inviting a friend to dinner that evening, and receive an RSVP in time to prepare.

The messages shared and the beautiful scenes combine to create the timeless appeal of postcards as a collectible. Most importantly, history is recorded by the pictures of the times, moments in time reflecting an alluring past.

Dating Postcards

Pioneer Era (1893-1898): Most pioneer cards in today's collections begin with cards placed on sale at the Columbian Exposition in Chicago on May 1, 1893. These were illustrations on government printed postal cards and privately printed souvenir cards. The government cards had the printed one-cent stamp, while souvenir cards required a two-cent adhesive postage stamp to be applied. Writing was not permitted on the address side of the card.

Private Mailing Card Era (1898-1901): On May 19, 1898, private printers were granted permission, by an act of Congress, to print and sell cards that bore the inscription "Private Mailing Card." A one-cent adhesive stamp was required. A dozen or more American printers began to take postcards seriously. Writing was still not permitted on the back.

Post Card Era - Undivided Back (1901-1907): New U.S. postal regulations on December 24, 1901 stipulated that the words "Post Card" should be printed at the top of the address side of privately printed cards. Government-issued cards were to be designated as "Postal Cards." Writing was still not permitted on the address side. In this era, private citizens began to take black and white photographs and have them printed on paper with post card backs.

Early Divided Back Era (1907-1914): Postcards with a divided back were permitted in Britain in 1902, but not in the U.S. until March 1, 1907. The address was to be written on the right side; the left side was for writing messages. Many millions of cards were published in this era. Up to this point, most postcards were printed in Germany, which was far ahead of the United States in the use of lithographic processes. With the advent of World War I, the supply of postcards for American consumption switched from Germany to England and the United States.

White Border Era (1915-1930): Most United States postcards were printed during this period. To save ink, publishers left a clear border around the view, thus these postcards are referred to as "White Border" cards. The relatively high cost of labor, along with inexperience and changes in public taste, resulted in the production of poor quality cards during this period. Furthermore, strong competition in a narrowing market caused many publishers to go out of business.

Linen Era (1930-1944): New printing processes allowed printing on postcards with high rag content that created a textured finish. These cheap cards allowed the use of gaudy dyes for coloring.

Photochrome Era (1945 to date): "Chrome" postcards began to dominate the scene soon after the Union Oil Company placed them in its western service stations in 1939. Mike Roberts pioneered with his "WESCO" cards soon after World War II. Three-dimensional postcards also appeared in this era.

Example of a postcard with an undivided back. Senders could only write the address on this side of the card. Any message needed to be written on the front of the card along with the picture.

Sample of a postcard with a divided back. Senders were allowed to put an address on the right-hand side of the postcard and a message on the left side.

The Missions

San Diego was home to Native Americans for thousands of years before its discovery by Juan Rodriguez Cabrillo in 1542. Sixty years later, another Spanish explorer, Sebastian Viscaino, came to the land, naming it San Diego, after Saint Didacus of Alcala. San Diego was claimed by Spain, although settlement did not begin until 1768. In April 1769, a group of Franciscan Friars came to shore and began to establish the California missions, the first of which was the San Diego de Alcala mission, led by Father Junipero Serra. This was the birthplace of Christianity in the West.

This hand-tinted depiction of the old mission at San Diego highlights the palm trees and agriculture for which the region is famous. In the beginning days of the mission, a shortage of fresh water, farmable land, and frequent skirmishes with Native Americans caused the mission to be relocated. The history of San Diego reflects that of the mission. Until 1831, the church was controlled by the Franciscans. However, when Mexico won its independence from Spain in 1831, they gave the mission to Sanitago Arguello. The United States eventually acquired the land in 1853.

Cancelled 1911, $4-6

Founded in 1769 by Father Junipero Serra, the Mission de Alcala was the first in California.

Circa 1907, $4-6

This postcard shows the mission before
the bell tower was added.

Circa 1907, $4-6

Bell Tower, Mission San Diego de Alcala. The bells ring once
a year on the mission's birthday. On the back: "Founded by
Fra Junipero Serra, July 16, 1769, this was the first of the
chain of twenty-one Franciscan missions built in California.
The mission suffered a number of attacks by Indians and
was practically destroyed in 1775. It was rebuilt and con-
tinued in active service until the Mexican secularization in
1829. The Mission was re-stored in 1930."

Circa 1940s, $4-6

Throughout the 1800s and early 1900s, the Mission served many purposes. In 1847, the United States Cavalry used the building as barracks and stables. From 1892 to 1909, the Sisters of Saint Joseph Carondolet conducted a Native American children's school in the mission. The many ownership changes and uses left the mission in near ruins by 1930.

Cancelled 1910, $4-6

San Diego Mission, San Diego, Cal.

716:—INNER COURT, MISSION SAN DIEGO DE ALCALA, C

© Herz

42391

716 Inner Court Mission San Diego de Alcala. The quadrangle design of the courtyard is common among the twenty-one missions in California. The Mission is still an active Catholic parish and was acknowledged by Pope Paul VI as a Minor Basilica.

Circa 1940s, $3-5

Junipero Serra Museum and Cross

735: - JUNIPERO SERRA MUSEUM, OLD TOWN, SAN DIEGO, CALIFORNIA

From the back: "The Junipero Serra Museum, overlooks the Valley of the Missions on Presidio Hill, where California began. It was presented to the City of San Diego by George W. Marston."

Circa 1940s, $3-5

From the back: "Housing the collections of the Pioneer Society and San Diego Historical Society, the Junipero Serra Museum is located in the beautiful Presidio Park, Old Town, San Diego. Here is also the Serra Cross made of old adobe bricks from the ruins of the original Spanish Presidio fort."

Cancelled 1949, $4-6

JUNIPERO SERRA MUSEUM, OLD TOWN, SAN DIEGO, CALIFORNIA—39

49:—Junipero Serra Historical Museum, Presidio Hill, San Diego, Calif.

From the back: "Junipero Serra Museum was dedicated to the founder of California Missions on this hill July 15, 1769. Padre Junipero Serra and the soldiers of Spain dedicated the mission, San Diego de Acala. This museum in all its beauty and simplicity has become a landmark since its erection on Presidio Hill. Almost as soon as a ship enters the harbor, the passengers can sight this imposing memorial to the vision of our early Spanish Californians."

Cancelled 1930, $4-6

4347. SERRA MONUMENT, OLD TOWN, SAN DIEGO, CALIF.

FRAY JUNIPERO SERRA

An aerial view of Presidio Park shows the Junipero Serra Museum and Cross.

Circa 1940s, $4-6

JUNIPERO SERRA MUSEUM
PRESIDIO PARK
SAN DIEGO, CAL.

From the back: "The Serra Monument was erected by the Order of Panama, San Diego, each member bringing an adobe brick form the old Mission de Alcala and placing it in position. A bronze tablet indicates the commemoration and the spot selected in where [sic] Fremont raised the first flag in California and the first cross was built by Father Serra." The cross was built in 1913.

Circa 1930s, $3-5

14

First American Flag

4371. Ramona's Marriage Place and Flag Monument, marking the spot where The U. S. Flag was first raised in Southern California, in 1846, San Diego, Cal.

The first American flag was raised in California on July 29, 1848. The Flag Monument marks the spot where an American flag replaced a Mexican flag that had been waving in the wind since Fr. Junipero Serra's arrival in 1769. "Ramona's Well" marked the marriage spot of a national heroine.

Circa 1915, $4-6

From the back: "The Plaza 'San Diego Viejo' is an historic landmark. It was established as the center of the Mexican Pueblo of San Diego, which elected its first Ayuntamiento in 1834. It was taken by American forces in November 1846. The Mexican flag was cut down by Senora Maria Antonia Machadoer de Silvas and the first American Flag was raised here in 1846 under enemy fire."

Circa 1940s, $3-5

734:- "PLAZA" WHERE THE FIRST AMERICAN FLAG IN CALIFORNIA WAS RAISED IN 1846

OLD TOWN, SAN DIEGO, CALIFORNIA   42409

Ramona's Marriage Place and Monument marking Spot American Flag was first raised in Southern Cal., San Diego

Ramona's Marriage Place, also known as Casa de Estidullo, can be seen in the background. This adobe structure was the only complete Spanish hacienda in Old Town and was made famous in a novel by Helen Hunt Jackson.

Circa 1910, $4-6

The Mexican cannon in the right corner was first installed when the Mission de Acala was moved to its current location.

Circa 1930, $4-6

Other Missions

The Mission San Antonio de Pala. From the back: "Mission San Antonio de Pala, North of San Diego, ... is not only noted for its unusual and picturesque campanile or bell tower, but it still has one of the largest native Indian congregations. The forefathers of many of the present attendants were among the original builders of this Mission when it was founded in 1816."

Cancelled 1940, $3-5

From the back: "Asistencia de San Antonio de Pala, San Diego County, is about twenty miles from San Luis Rey, to which it was attached. Its bell tower is the only distinguishing feature of the old establishment, distant from the beaten roads of travel. This is home to the remnants of the thousands of Indians who inhabited the surrounding country and who reverence [sic], even yet, the memories of the good Fathers who labored for their welfare."

Circa 1930s, $3-5

From the back: "First pepper tree in California, as seen from the ancient Arches, through the Portals of the Patio of Mission San Luis Rey. The remains of the Aqueducts in the foreground." At the writing of this book, the pepper tree was still growing there.

Circa 1930s, $2-4

18

At the Mission San Luis Rey, San Diego County, Cal.

MISSION SAN LUIS REY DE FRANCIA, SAN DIEGO COUNTY, CALIFORNIA·   M15

Mission San Luis Rey de Francia, the eighteenth mission in California, founded on June 13, 1798.

Circa 1920s, $3-5

Mission San Luis Rey took three years to build and was named for Saint Louis IX, king of France in 1798.

Circa 1905, $4-6

Old Town and Ramona's Legacy

Helen Hunt Jackson was a passionate writer, determined to make a positive difference in the life of the Native American in the mid 1800s. Her first novel, A Century of Dishonor, railed about the deplorable treatment of the Indians and called for fair and humane policies. Her activism led her to Southern California to examine the plight of the Californian Indian. While traveling throughout the state, she researched the Indians and sent letters and reports to Congress. Upon returning to the East Coast, Jackson decided to write a novel about her experiences. Using a young Native American woman raised in a mission-style home in San Diego as protagonist, Jackson tried to charge the emotions of her readers to take action for the Native Americans. Ramona, a Story was published in 1884 and enjoyed almost instant success. The novel, instead of drawing attention and sympathy for Native Americans, drew tourists and crowds to Old Town, San Diego. Readers, believing Ramona lived in the Casa de Estudillo, visited the location. The postcards of Ramona's Marriage Place celebrate this fictional heroine and allow Helen Hunt Jackson's novel and passion to continue. They also document the incredible tourism phenomena the novel helped to launch, a virtual industry that helped define and expand the city of San Diego. The Ramona legacy continues, with theater and tourist attractions dedicated to this romantic, fictional heroine.

From the back: "The tenth year of the Ramona Pageant Play. Presented by the people of Hemet and San Jacinto, Riverside County California. The phenomenal success and approval of the thousands of spectators who witnessed this play in previous years demand a continuance of California's more colorful outdoor drama. For three weekends, April 23-24; April 30, May 1; and May 7-8. Play starts at 3 p.m." The pageant still takes place today in the Ramona Amphitheater in Hemet, California, the longest-running production of its kind. A cast of over 400 people reenact the famous novel.

Cancelled 1936, $4-6

RAMONA AT HER HUSBAND'S GRAVE.

In Helen Hunt Jackson's famous novel, Alessandro Assis was Ramona's first husband, a sheep herder who stole her heart. After his death, Ramona married her stepbrother, Felipe Moreno. Here she is shown mourning the loss of her true love.

Circa 1905, $3-5

A front view of the small home established as the residence of the fictional heroine of Helen Hunt Jackson's 1884 novel Ramona.

Circa 1910, $4-6

From the back: "Estudello house at Old Town, San Diego, California, where Ramona signed the marriage register. This quaint old ruin has been fully restored and is now the only Spanish Grande's home in the United States. The Patio is a magnificent flower garden, and its tiled floors and roofs, hide-bound rafters, and adobe walls charm the many tourists who visit it daily. The collection of paintings is a century old and the rooms contain many curios."

Circa 1915, $3-5

Despite the heading on this card, Ramona never lived in this home. Two generations of the Estudillo family called this adobe structure "home" in the mid 1800s. After leaving the home in 1887, the furniture was stripped and sold and the area was left in disrepair.

Cancelled 1930, $4-6

62:—RAMONA'S MARRIAGE PLACE BEFORE RESTORATION, SAN DIEGO, CALIF.

The adobe home was restored in 1910 by the Spreckles family and remains a popular tourist destination. Spreckles renamed the Casa de Estudel-lo "Ramona's Marriage Place" to attract tourists to visit, a journey that required them to ride the Spreckles-owned streetcar service.

Circa 1920s, $3-5

56B:—"Cactus Garden" at Ramona's Marriage Place, Old Town, San Diego, Calif.

A cactus garden at Ramona's Marriage Place in Old Town, San Diego.

Circa 1920s, $3-5

Prior to restoration, the courtyard as seen by the first tourists lured to this spot.

Cancelled 1908, $4-6

The courtyard at Ramona's Home is a typical feature of Spanish architecture. The sender of this cards writes, "San Diego is a lovely little place and just this time of year, the flowers are all in bloom."

Cancelled 1911, $3-5

The bright colors and patterns of the rugs along the patio highlight the California or mission style that Jackson wrote about, the popularity of her novel helping to spur the spread of "California Colonial" style.

Circa 1930s, $4-6

726:—THE CHAPEL IN WHICH RAMONA WAS MARRIED. RAMONA'S MARRIAGE PLACE.

© Herz

OLD TOWN. SAN DIEGO. CALIFORNIA.

The Chapel where the fictional Ramona was married. When the old mission churches were falling apart from age and lack of funds, the Estudillo family allowed the town to use a room in their home as a chapel until the mission church was safe again. As the Ramona myth grew, people believed the chapel existed inside the home.

Circa 1940s, $4-6

PATIO, RAMONA'S MARRIAGE PLACE, OLD TOWN, SAN DIEGO, CALIFORNIA—56

From the back: "Ramona's Marriage Place is the old Spanish adobe known as Casa de Estudillo. Built in 1825, it is a show place and now houses a large collection of Spanish, Indian, and early American antiques."

Cancelled 1947, $2-4

24

4374 THE WISHING WELL AT RAMONA'S MARRIAGE PLACE, OLD TOWN, SAN DIEGO. CALIF

The wishing well at Ramona's Marriage Place. Above the well reads, "Quaff ye the waters of Ramona's well; Good Luck they bring and secrets tell, Blessed were they by sandaled Friar. So drink and wish for thy desire." Despite the old saying and lure, the wishing well was part of the renovations by Spreckles.

Circa 1930s, $2-4

67:—The Old Spanish Oven, Ramona's Marriage Place, San Diego, Calif.

First Stage in California at Ramona's Marriage Place, San Diego

An "old" Spanish oven was added to tantalize tourists.

Cancelled 1937, $2-4

The first stage coach in California found a final resting place at Ramona's.

Cancelled 1919, $3-5

The Bay

With its natural harbor, San Diego is home to the only West Coast shipyard adequate for building and repairing big ocean-going vessels. The deep, clement harbor has also proven perfect for naval activities and has served the country in this capacity for decades.

Point Loma has a spectacular view of the ocean and of the city. The community is on a peninsula that juts out into the Pacific.

Circa 1940s, $4-6

A very early view of San Diego and Bay, dating back to when messages had to be written on the front of a card. This one was never used, and has been carefully preserved.

Circa 1905, $5-7

3804 Birds'-eye View Looking West from Timpkin Building, San Diego, California

Birds' eye view looking west
from Timpkin Building over the
bustle of the city circa 1915.

Circa 1915, $7-9

This view of San Diego was seen
by thousands of pilots from the
U.S. Naval Air force.

Circa 1940s, $5-7

4546—PBY Plane in Flight over San Diego, California

1B-H1010

The Municipal Piers

4591. MUNICIPAL PIERS, SAN DIEGO, CALIF.

106136

4655. Steamer at Municipal Pier, San Diego, Cal.

Boats, yachts, and cruise ships docked along the two long piers in the San Diego Harbor.

Circa 1930s, $7-9

A steamer docked at Municipal pier. The pier was built in the early twentieth century.

Circa 1920s, $8-10

1174 — YACHTING ON SAN DIEGO BAY, CALIFORNIA.

**Yachting on the
San Diego Bay.**

Circa 1915, $4-6

3807 Birds'-eye View of San Diego. California, from San Diego Bay

**This aerial view of San Diego shows the piers jutting out like fingers into the
warm bay.**

Circa 1930s, $7-9

**Quarantine Station, Entrance to San Diego
Harbor, San Diego, California.**

327

**Ballast Point, under military control, is the entrance to the bay, keeping San
Diegans and Californians safe.**

Circa 1905, $6-8

Sea Gulls, San Diego, Cal.

A bird's-eye view of the harbor.

Circa 1910, $5-7

Bay of San Diego, Cal.

A view across the bay.

Cancelled 1913, $5-7

SAN DIEGO AND CORONADO FERRY, SAN DIEGO, CALIFORNIA—80

The Coronado Ferry was a highlight of the El Coronado Hotel. John D. Spreckles bought the boat not just to get guests to the hotel quickly, but to make sure every moment of their trip was enjoyable. Many people loved the ferry ride across the bay as much as their time in Coronado.

Cancelled 1951, $8-10

802 SAN DIEGO AND CORONADO FERRY, WITH PART OF U. S. FLEET IN REAR.

9-2063

"Laura" writes on the back of this card: "This is the boat that takes me across the Bay, where I go to San Diego. The upper deck is for passengers and the lower deck for cars. You can see a few U.S. Navy boats anchored in the bay."

Circa 1940s, $7-9

The Military

San Diego once had the nickname "Navy Town USA." The following postcards and captions show how the city earned that moniker. San Diego is the westernmost city in the continental United States, with various geographical attributes that lend themselves to this type of activity, such as the nearby ocean for Naval exercises and wide open deserts and mountains for air exercises. After Pearl Harbor, protection from Japan and attacks on the homeland became a major concern and San Diego was deemed a key defensive point for the country.

2379 – MILITARY ROAD TO FORT ROSECRANS, POINT LOMA, SAN DIEGO, CALIFORNIA.
SHOWING WHARF OF NEW COALING STATION AND QUARANTINE STATION.

Military Road to Fort Rosecrans, Point Loma, San Diego California showing wharf and new coaling station and quarantine station. The U.S Naval Coaling Station was established in 1907 off the shores of Point Loma. This fueling station led to permanent military stations that greatly contributed to the advancement of San Diego.

Cancelled 1912, $5-7

Fort Rosencrans, Showing Officers Quarters, San Diego, Cal.

The Army established Fort Rosecrans in 1899. It was transferred to the Navy in 1959.

Circa 1915, $5-7

A 60-foot granite monument stands in memory of the 60 men killed and 40 injured when two boilers exploded aboard the U.S. Navy gunboat Bennington on July 21, 1905.

Circa 1910, $5-7

4392. Bennington Monument, San Diego, Cal.

48:—U. S. NAVY FLEET OF DESTROYERS COMING INTO BAY. SAN DIEGO. CALIFORNIA.

© Herz 1701

In 1907, "The Great White Fleet," a fleet of sixteen new battleships and between fourteen and sixteen thousand sailors set out to sail around the world. San Diego was their first stop.

Circa 1920s, $5-7

near Pt. Loma, San Diego, Calif.

17637

An overview of the U.S. Naval Training Station. The Navy established the base in 1912 with only three airplanes and three fliers. Rockwell Field and an aviation school were formed by the Army Signal Corps on Thanksgiving of that same year.

Circa 1920s, $4-6

4580—U. S. Naval Training Station, San Diego, California

9A-H2257

From the back: "Recruits standing by for inspection at the Naval Training Station, San Diego, California, on a Saturday morning. They are formed in a quadrangle known as Paul Jones Court, named after their illustrious predecessor, John Paul Jones. All recruits from the Western part of the United States are sent to this station before being assigned to the Fleet."

Circa 1940s, $6-8

4508   ADMINISTRATION BUILDING, U. S. NAVAL AIR STATION, NORTH ISLAND, SAN DIEGO, CALIFORNIA

1A-H497

San Diego was once referred to as "Navytown USA." The constant flow of sailors, other military personnel and their families throughout the base was a significant factor in the growth of the city.

Circa 1940s, $6-8

35

4452. ENTRANCE U.S. NAVAL TRAINING STATION, SAN D...

Entrance to the U.S. Naval Training Station.

Circa 1920s, $5-7

Looking Southwest toward the parade grounds on the U.S. Marine Corps Base.

Circa 1940s, $4-6

837M   LOOKING SOUTHWEST TOWARD PARADE GROUND, U. S. MARINE CORPS BASE. SAN DIEGO, CALIFORNIA

E-4428

843   MAIN GATE. NAVAL AIR STATION. SAN DIEGO. CALIFORNIA

E-5062

The main gate at the Naval Air Station.

Circa 1940s, $5-7

831M   BARRACKS AND PARADE GROUND. LOOKING WEST. U. S. MARINE CORPS BASE. SAN DIEGO. CALIFORNIA

E-4422

The Spanish-style buildings of the Naval Training Station were designed by Bertram Goodhue, who also designed many of the buildings in the Balboa Park for the Panama-California Exposition. Additional military buildings were designed by Stevenson, including the Army-Navy YMCA in downtown San Diego.

Circa 1930s, $5-7

4599 AIRCRAFT MANEUVERS OVER NORTH ISLAND, SAN DIEGO, CALIFORNIA

6A-H2629

Nicknamed the "Air Capital of the West," San Diego's skies continue as busy training grounds as well as a hub of people transport. From the back: "Directly across the bay from the business district of San Diego is North Island, the home of Uncle Sam's greatest aeronautical operating units. This activity keeps the air above San Diego literally full of different types of planes."

Circa 1930s, $5-7

In 1941, The San Diego Naval Air Station began training pilots for the U.S. Air Force.

Circa 1940s, $5-7

CONSOLIDATED AIRCRAFT CORP., SAN DIEGO, CALIFORNIA—9

Mid-century San Diego was home port to approximately 150 of Uncle Sam's warships, including light cruisers, aircraft carriers, destroyers, submarines, repair ships, floating dry docks, tenders, oilers, etc.

Circa 1940s, $6-8

4520   U. S. NAVY PLANE CARRIER AT ANCHOR—LOOKING UP BROADWAY, SAN DIEGO, CALIFORNIA

3A-H1374

300A —SHORE LEAVE ON THE PACIFIC COAST, SAN DIEGO

The city of San Diego became a popular off-base destination for servicemen, strengthening the city's economy through income and business. Despite the closure of the NTC in 1997, some 103,000 Navy and Marine personnel are still based in San Diego, along with 26,000 civilian Navy employees, and 60,000 Navy retirees.

Cancelled 1943, $6-8

U.S. Naval Hospital, Balboa Park

4450. U.S. NAVAL HOSPITAL, BALBOA PARK, SAN DIEGO, CALIF.

The U.S. Naval Hospital in Balboa Park was constructed at a cost of over two million dollars
to provide for the sick and injured officers and men of the U.S. Fleet. The hospital building is
another example of Spanish mission influence by Bertram Goodhue, a New York architect who
also designed buildings for the Naval Training Center.

Cancelled 1925, $5-7

3C:—United States Naval Hospital, Balboa Park, San Diego, Calif.

This aerial view of the hospital shows the large courtyards and adobe roofs that are staples of Spanish mission designs. The original plans called for four groups of wards for patients, an administration building, and a supply store. The building was to encompass seventeen acres of what was known as Inspiration Point and cost one million dollars.

Cancelled 1933, $6-8

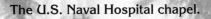

The U.S. Naval Hospital chapel.

Circa 1940s, $6-8

U.S. NAVAL HOSPITAL CHAPEL, SAN DIEGO, CALIF.—18

Skylines and Streetscapes

Downtown

Fifth Street and Broadway are the main focus of San Diego's historic downtown postcards since they were, and remain, busy sections of the city. Today, major stores and restaurants adorn these streets and the buildings are taller.

Lined with old-fashioned buildings, palm trees, and bustling businesses, Broadway was the main attraction in San Diego.

Circa 1940s, $7-9

From the back: "Running east from the Embarcadero, through the heart of downtown San Diego, Broadway is a principal thoroughfare. On each side are many of the city's outstanding buildings, hotels, theaters, stores and other business institutions."

Circa 1940s, $8-10

BROADWAY, SAN DIEGO, CALIFORNIA—23

Another view of Broadway, a distinctive bowling alley dominating the foreground.

Circa 1940s, $9-11

From the back: "This view shows one of the busiest sections of San Diego. In the foreground is the U.S. Grant Hotel, fireproof and remarkable in its completeness." D Street was later renamed Broadway.

Circa 1915, $12-14

Broadway looking east, showing Spreckles Theatre and Central Mortgage Building in the foreground and U.S. Grant Hotel in background.

Circa 1920s, $12-14

From the back: "Fifth Avenue is a busy thoroughfare in the heart of downtown San Diego. Here are located many of the city's leading department stores, specialty shops and office buildings." This area is now referred to as the Gas Lamp Quarter and is known for great shopping and dinning.

Circa 1950s, $8-10

An early view of Fifth street looking south.

Circa 1905, $13-15

Fifth st. Looking South, San Diego, Cal.

413 — FIFTH STREET, LOOKING NORTH FROM F, SAN DIEGO, CALIFORNIA.

Fifth street looking north from F Street, trolley tracks running down the center.

Circa 1915, $13-15

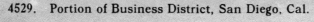

3821 Looking North on Sixth Street, San Diego. California

Looking North on Sixth Street.

Cancelled 1913, $12-14

An aerial view of the
business district.

Copyright 1911, $10-12

4529. Portion of Business District, San Diego, Cal.

POINT LOMA

U.S. AVIATION FIELD   SOUTH-DAKOTA   PENNSYLVANIA

CALIFORNIA

4510   A PORTION OF THE BUSINESS AREA OF SAN DIEGO, CALIFORNIA, BALBOA PARK IN THE DISTANCE

A later overview of the city.

Circa 1940s, $7-9

DOWNTOWN SAN DIEGO, CALIFORNIA—5

From the back: "San Diego, with its population
of 300,000 is America's Number One defense
city. Here the Army, Navy and Marine Corps
have large operating and training bases and
the aircraft industry has developed to a high
degree. This modern business district provides excellent services for the citizens of the
community."

Circa 1940s, $05-012

4566.   U. S. Post Office and Custom House, San Diego, Calif.

A view of the U.S. Post Office and Custom House. The combination of classical architecture mixed with Spanish colonial revival reflects the diverse nature of San Diego. This building was commissioned in 1913 to be the first Federal building in San Diego in anticipation of the Panama Exposition and growth of the city.

Circa 1915, $7-9

The tower of the City Hall and Civic Center reaches one hundred fifty feet into the air, or five stories above the roof. It was originally to be two hundred feet, but concerns about the local airfield kept it down. From the back: "The first unit of the Civic Center for the combined city and county of San Diego is this modern Administration building located on San Diego's water front. This $1,000,000 edifice is used jointly by the city and the county governments."

Cancelled 1950, $7-9

4567. Santa Fe Railroad Depot, San Diego, Cal.

4569. Union Depot, Atchison, Topeka & Santa Fe Ry., San Diego & Arizona Ry., San Diego, Cal.

Just like the Customs Building, the Santa Fe Railroad Depot was built in celebration of the Panama–California International Exposition in 1915 and demonstrates Spanish colonial architecture. It was designed by architects John R. Bakewell and Arthur Brown, Jr., and built by Atchinson, Topeka and Santa Fe Railways.

Circa 1930s, $10-12 each

4547—Santa Fe Station, San Diego, California

IB-HI011

This has always
been a busy station. A later
view boasts a streamlined train unloading
passengers, and a trolley ready to whisk them off to view
the city's delights. Automobile travel downshifted the need for trains.
The peak of rail travel from Santa Fe Union Station was 1924, but shortly
after that, lines began to close and depots were abandoned. The San Diego
Arizona line was shut down in 1951.

Circa 1940s, $7-9

While the station looks
tranquil in this postcard,
it was once the second
busiest Amtrak rail cor-
ridor and bus terminus.
The building was pre-
served and added to the
National Register of His-
toric Buildings in 1972.

Circa 1920s, $5-7

71992 SANTA FE STATION, SAN DIEGO, CALIFORNIA

MERCY HOSPITAL, SAN DIEGO, CALIFORNIA—75

From the back: "A fine example of the many buildings to be seen in San Diego, is the Mercy Hospital, a nurses' training school. Here, in this city, which is a far-flung panorama of superlative grandeur, one will find many such beautiful buildings."

Circa 1930s, $6-8

99:—Mercy Hospital, San Diego, Calif.

Begun as a mere dispensary in the late 1800s, Mercy Hospital has been through a number of transformations that provided needed medical care to the community, and medical training for nurses. It is now known as Scripps Mercy Surgery Pavilion.

Cancelled 1926, $6-8

THE COURT HOUSE, SAN DIEGO, CALIFORNIA—79   MEDICO-DENTAL BUILDING   CORTEZ HOTE

From the back: "Located in downtown San Diego, the County Court House houses municipal and superior courts, law library, office of the district attorney, county clerk and other county offices."

Circa 1940s, $5-7

4267. Spreckles Theatre, San Diego, Cal.

The Spreckles Theatre opened on August 23, 1912 with a production of "Bought and Paid For" by George Broadhurst. It billed itself as the first modern play house west of the Mississippi.

Circa 1915, $6-8

"THE SAN DIEGO ARMED SERVICES YMCA

From the back: "The San Diego Armed Services YMCA is the largest YMCA in the World serving men and women in uniform."

Circa 1940s, $5-7

FREE PUBLIC LIBRARY, SAN DIEGO, CALIFORNIA.

The Free Public Library in San Diego.

Cancelled 1910, $5-7

54

Education

This San Diego High School was built in 1907 to make room for a quickly growing population. Understandably, students referred to their high school as the "Old Grey Castle."

Cancelled 1908, $7-9

San Diego High School, Cal.

4572. The High School, San Diego, Cal.

The 'Castle' soon needed more room. In 1912, a home economics and science building were started and in 1915 a large stadium was added as well. The 'Castle' remained until 1976.

Cancelled 1921, $7-9

4164. The High School, National City, San Diego, Cal.

The High School in National City, San Diego.

Circa 1915, $7-9

State Normal School, San Diego, Cal.

Copyright 1910, Passmore.

The State Normal School opened in 1897 for training for elementary school teachers, the first graduating class boasting only seven instructors and ninety-one students.

Copyright 1910, $7-9

COPR. DETROIT PUBLISHING CO.

13593 NORMAL SCHOOL, SAN DIEGO, CALIF.

Historians contest which architect designed The State Normal School – either Irving Gill or W.S. Hebbard. The latter mentored Gill in his early career.

Circa 1920s, $7-9

Now San Diego State University, San Diego State College advanced from a two-year program for teachers to a four-year liberal arts college in 1931. Much of the architecture on the seventeen-acre campus was modeled in The Spanish Revival tradition, or mission style.

Circa 1940s, $5-7

740:—STATE COLLEGE, SAN DIEGO, CALIFORNIA.

© Herz

Residential Areas

Residence Street, San Diego, Cal.—23

Street Scene at El Cajon, San Diego Co., Cal.

The beautiful climate and economic potential of San Diego attracted many Americans. This photograph shows a residential street in under a clear blue sky, lined with palm trees.

Circa 1920s, $6-8

The view of El Cajon Boulevard today is quite different from the peaceful, empty street depicted here. El Cajon is one of the major commercial strips in San Diego.

Cancelled 1908, $8-10

4630. Residence of Mme. Schumann Heink, Grossmont, near San Diego, Cal.

Residence of Mme. Schumann Heink in Grossmont, near San Diego. Madame Schuman Heink was a famous opera singer who mesmerized America with her powerful voice and charitable heart from 1898 to 1903. She performed at Balboa Park for the Panama-California Exposition.

Cancelled 1921, $5-7

A RESIDENCE STREET IN SAN DIEGO, CALIFORNIA

A card promotes the life in San Diego. From the back: "To have a home in San Diego is to have a garden, with no limit to its plants and flowers."

Circa 1910, $5-7

Arthur Putnam, a famous animal sculptor, lived in this spacious home in the outskirts of San Diego in the 1910s. Putnam studied sculptor all over Europe and California. He developed a career-ending brain tumor in 1909.

Cancelled 1908, $5-7

W. H. Putnam's Residence. San Diego, Cal.

J. C. Packard, San Diego, Cal.

3866—Scripps Residence, La Jolla, San Diego, California.

Also called Moulton Villa, this home of Ellen Browning Scripps had rooms for entertaining as well as relaxing. It housed a library full of books on natural history. The home, designed by San Diegan architect Irving Gill, was destroyed by fire. The site is now home to the La Jolla Museum of Contemporary Art.

Circa 1910, $4-6

The Theosophical Institute

59:—Buildings of the Theosophical Society, San Diego, Calif.

Theosophical Institute, Point Loma, San Diego, Calif.

Among the beliefs and practices of the Theosophical Institute was self sufficiency through agriculture. Theosophists brought avocado and orange crops to the southern California region. Both of which remain the region's largest crops to this day.

Circa 1915, $4-6

The Theosophical Institute in San Diego was founded by Kathryn Tingley, who bought land there in 1897. She arranged to have the buildings face south and chose the most western point of the North American continent all in order to be closer to the center of their beliefs, India.

Circa 1920s, $3-5

The entryway to the Theosophical Institute. The Theosophical Institute is now part of the Point Loma Nazarene University.

Circa 1910, $4-6

Theosophical Institute, Point Loma, San Diego, Cal.

U.S. Grant Hotel

U. S. Grant Hotel. San Diego, Cal.

This hotel was built and operated by U.S. Grant Jr. in honor of his illustrious father Gen. Ulysses S. Grant.

Circa 1910, $6-8

Like many others, the Grant family came to San Diego seeking a fresh start. Ulysses Jr. had suffered many financial setbacks in the East. His wife, Fannie Chaffee Grant, daughter of a wealthy Colorado Senator, struggled with respiratory problems and felt the warm climate would improve her health.

Circa 1910, $6-8

4292. U. S. Grant Hotel looking down D Street, San Diego Cal.

Alonzo E. Horton, also known as the "Father of New Town San Diego," bought 960 acres of what is now downtown San Diego. A wealthy merchant from San Francisco, Horton had a keen eye for development and real estate. In 1870, he built the first luxury hotel in San Diego, the Horton Hotel and The Horton Plaza across D Street. However, Fannie Chaffee Grant bought the property in 1895. Her husband, Ulysses Grant Jr., after working at the hotel for several years, demolished the three story wood structure to make way for his five-hundred room luxury hotel.

Circa 1915, $9-11

Lobby from Main Entrance, U. S. Grant Hotel. San Diego. Cal.

A view of the Main Entrance Lobby. The U.S. Grant opened its doors for the first time on October 15, 1910. Construction was halted several times. The earthquake of 1906 caused a lumber shortage and hindered development. Financial strains also slowed the five-year project. The $1.5 million hotel had 350 rooms with private baths, a 9th floor ballroom, swimming pools with salt water straight from the sea, and "Ladies Foyers," suites that provided guests on the first floor with private entrances.

Copyright 1910, $6-8

BALL ROOM, U. S. GRANT HOTEL, SAN DIEGO, CAL.

The Grand Ballroom is shown, garlanded in tropical greenery. The Grand Ballroom was able to accommodate five hundred people. On opening night, October 15 1910, almost 20,000 gathered for the grand opening. The only one not in attendance was the owner Ulysses Grant Jr., who had been called away to New York on business.

Cancelled 1912, $6-8

THE PALM COURT, U. S. GRANT HOTEL, SAN DIEGO, CAL. COPYRIGHT ENO & MATTESON 1910.

The Palm Court once bordered the east and west wings of the hotel.

Circa 1915, $6-8

Another romantic and opulent feature of the U.S Grant Hotel were the Roof Garden esplanades. Guests could enjoy views of the harbor from the two half-acre verandas.

Circa 1915, $5-7

Night Scene from the Roof Garden, U. S. Grant Hotel, San Diego, Cal.
COPYRIGHT ENO & MATTESON 1910.

The Plaza

4676 Plaza Park Showing L.J. Wilde Electric Fountain, U.S. Weather Kiosk, U.S. Grant Hotel, and Union Building. The sender of this postcard wrote: "This is a very pretty park and at night this electric fountain changes all colors."

Circa 1910, $5-7

Designed by Irving J. Gill, this fountain was the centerpiece of the Horton Plaza, and the city. It was the first to use electricity to project colored water in the evening. Thomas Edison was said to have helped on the engineering of the fountain. Gill modeled it after the monument to the Greek God Lysicrates in Athens, circa 334. B.C.

Cancelled 1911, $2-4

NIGHT VIEW OF PLAZA, SAN DIEGO, CALIFORNIA—68

50:—THE PLAZA, SAN DIEGO, CALIFORNIA.

Located in what is now known as the Gaslamp Quarter, the Horton Plaza is in the heart of San Diego. Named for a legendary city founder, the park opened in conjunction with the U.S. Grant Hotel across the street. Civic buildings, including the Union Building, were planned around the plaza.

Circa 1930s, $7-9

The Horton Plaza is now a major shopping center with high-end stores. It looks very different from the original town center envisioned by Horton in the early twentieth century. From the back: "In the center of busy downtown San Diego, the Plaza is a colorful spot. Surrounding it are many of the city's prominent hotels, theatres, and buildings."

Cancelled 1946, $7-9

The men in this postcard image could be looking at the weather charts, posted in the U.S Weather Bureau Kiosk or discussing the current events in the city. People would come to parts of Plaza Park to speak about subjects such as women's suffrage, the evils of drink, and other societal issues. The park was never intended to have more than fifty visitors.

Cancelled 1911, $7-9

2374 — PLAZA AND U. S. WEATHER BUREAU KIOSK, SAN DIEGO, CALIFORNIA.

Other Prominent Hotels

4595   A PORTION OF SAN DIEGO, CALIFORNIA, SKYLINE SHOWING EL CORTEZ HOTEL AND SPRECKELS BUILDING

123730

This panoramic view shows the prominence of the El Cortez Hotel, one of San Diego's first "skyscrapers" built to command a view of the city, bay, and surrounding country. The Sky Room atop the tower was a much-touted attraction.

Circa 1920s, $5-7

Another feature of the El Cortez was the Don Room. Modeled after the majestic Spanish ships, the room hosted many galas and social events.

Cancelled 1940, $5-7

FAMOUS DON ROOM, EL CORTEZ HOTEL
SAN DIEGO, CALIFORNIA

THE SAN DIEGO HOTEL, SAN DIEGO, CALIF.

92787

Built by John D. Spreckles, the Hotel San Diego was located on Broadway and Union Streets. It boasted four hundred rooms, a coffee shop, and cocktail lounge. The hotel has since been demolished.

Circa 1920s, $6-8

Stratford Inn, Del Mar, near San Diego, Cal.

The Stratford Inn was part of a vision by realtor Ed Fletcher and newspaper man E.W. Scripps. A highway was built to reach the resort hotel and homes since it was located outside the city.

Circa 1915, $6-8

The Stratford's secluded location and Del Mar's resort reputation enticed many of the Hollywood elite to motor down for quick vacations. Many similar resorts and business grew on this reputation.

Circa 1920s, $5-7

STRATFORD INN, DEL MAR, SAN DIEGO COUNTY, CALIFORNIA

69

GENTLEMEN'S WRITING ROOM. HOTEL SANDFORD
SAN DIEGO, CAL.

andford, San Diego, Cal.

ENTRANCE, FOYER.
HOTEL SANDFORD,
SAN DIEGO, CAL.

Three views of the Sanford Hotel. From the backs: "Under the Personal management of F.S. Sanford, formerly manager of the Majestic Hotel of New York City; also the famous Grand Hotel of Yokohama Japan."

Circa 1915, $7-9 for first card, $6-8 for others

Maryland Hotel,
San Diego, California.

The Maryland Hotel is one of the last buildings left in San Diego that was designed by W.S. Hebbard. Built to command F Street between Sixth and Seventh streets, this hotel was one of the firsts to offer bathrooms connected to the rooms and clothes closets.

Circa 1920s, $7-9

123729

The Pickwick Hotel promoted its two hundred fifty outside rooms, all with private baths. In addition to being place of respite for thousands of travelers, the Pickwick Hotel was also home to one of the first commercial radio stations in San Diego. One can see the large antenna in the background.

Cancelled 1934, $7-9

La Valencia opened in 1926. It was a small inn until 1928 when owners MacArthur Gorton and Roy B. Wiltsie opened an eight-story addition with hotel-style rooms, balcony and lounges. Throughout the twentieth century, La Valencia's reputation of luxury and service attracted movie stars and celebrities. Visitors could escape into the La Jolla coves to enjoy the beautiful beaches or look East toward gentle mountains.

Circa 1950s, $5-7

LA VALENCIA HOTEL — LA JOLLA, CALIFORNIA

90830

Balboa Park and The Expo

In 1868, the City of San Diego set aside a magnanimous 1,400 acres designated as park land. Despite years of pressure to lease and develop, the city has managed to hold on to all but about 322 of those acres. Through the years, the park has served as a lush garden for Victorians, site of the glorious Panama-California Exposition of 1915, and home to the world-acclaimed San Diego Zoo.

The Laurel Street Entrance to Balboa Park. From the back: "the 1400 acre tract around which San Diego is built, is famous for its Spanish Renaissance buildings, many beauty spots, and luxuriant foliage that thrives in this near tropical climate."

Cancelled 1950, $3-5

Golden Hill Park is known today as a beautiful residential area. The residents enjoy proximity to what Is today Balboa Park. When it was called City Park, the residents undertook planting and maintaining the southeast corner near their home.

Circa 1915, $3-5

The beautiful buildings featured in this card were built for the Panama-California Exposition in 1915 to celebrate the opening of the Panama Canal and highlight the city of San Diego.

Circa 1915, $4-6

4408.   EL PRADO FROM WEST GATE, BALBOA PARK, SAN DIEGO, CALIF.

62442

Spanish Revival architecture was used extensively in the design of the park, supervised by architect Bertram Goodhue. The majestic thoroughfare of Spanish Renaissance structures culminates in the tower of the California Building in the distance.

Circa 1915, $5-7

S.D 41   PRADO, BALBOA PARK, SAN DIEGO, CALIFORNIA

Goodhue used the Exposition as a chance to create his own dream city. He used Muslim and Persian influences in the ornamental design of each building.

Copyright 1915, $7-9

105A:—The Tower of the California Bldg., Balboa Park,

San Diego, Calif.

4404. CALIFORNIA BUILDING, BALBOA PARK, SAN DIEGO, CALIF.

The tower and dome are mentioned extensively in literature about San Diego architecture. Bertram Goodhue designed the California Building and Bell Tower, drawing inspiration from the Moors of Spain, the towers of the Arab design and Spanish missions. San Diegans are very proud of the mixture of motifs. The mixture of Spanish Revival and Mexican color reflects the city's spirit and heritage.

Circa 1915, $3-5

Since its construction in 1914, the tower and the California Building have undergone many renovations and preservation efforts. The California Building is listed on the National Register of Historic Places.

Circa 1920s, $3-5

The elaborate buildings for the exposition were completed in less than three years. Groundbreaking ceremonies were in 1911 and the exposition opened in 1915. Many of the buildings were built solely for display purposes and not meant to last. After the exposition, many of the buildings were renovated, remodeled, or destroyed.

Canceled 1938, $4-6

Almost three million people attended the three day expo. The fair promoted San Diego as an ideal place to live. The purpose of the Expo was to "illustrate the progress and possibility of the human race…"

Cancelled 1915, $6-8

Exposition Buildings and Displays

The Panama Canal opened in 1914, creating countless possibilities for trade and travel from the Atlantic to the Pacific Oceans. San Diego would be the first northern Pacific port of call. The city, though small in population and weak in economy, wanted to celebrate the opening of the Canal and attract visitors. Three very important and influential San Diegans served on the planning board, U.S. Grant Jr., John D. Spreckles, and A.G. Spalding.

The buildings of the exposition were designed in Spanish Renaissance or Revival style, giving the park and city its unique personality. Visitors to the exposition were treated to foods from all over the world, a concert from a world-renowned opera singer, and many other delights. The Panama-California Exposition of 1915 was a huge success and San Diego made a name for itself as another city of significance in California. Two decades later, San Diego again threw open the doors for The San Diego Century-of-Progress Exposition, 1935-36. Many of the buildings from the first expo were saved and renovated, and the park got a new facelift and legacy.

The House of Hospitality and War Memorial Building , created for the Exposition of 1915-16.

Cancelled 1953, $3-5

The Palace of Food and Beverages, where "The world's choicest foods and viands, Americans finest fruits and vegetables" were on display for the Exposition. The beautiful building was preserved in the 1400-acre Balboa Park as an example of Spanish Renaissance architecture.

Cancelled 1953, $4-6

Palace of Better Housing and House of Hospitality From the back: "The masterly landscape, the loveliness of the gardens, and the harmonious perfection of architecture tend to make this the most beautiful of Expositions."

Circa 1915, $3-5

The Woman of Tehuantepec was added to the House of Hospitality patio in 1935, which was originally the Foreign Arts Building. This site served as the main reception area for the California–Pacific Exposition in 1936.

Circa 1930s, $4-6

63:—Fine Arts Gallery, Balboa Park, San Diego, Calif.

The Fine Arts Gallery in Balboa Park was a gift of Mr. and Mrs. Appleton Bridges. The structure was designed by William Templeton Johnson, a leading architect in San Diego who was also inspired by the Spanish Renaissance style.

Circa 1920s, $3-5

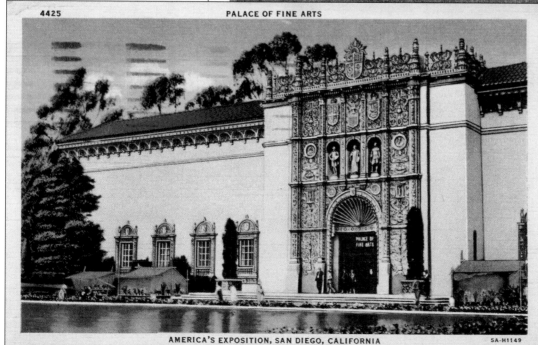

4425   PALACE OF FINE ARTS

AMERICA'S EXPOSITION, SAN DIEGO, CALIFORNIA   SA-H1149

In addition to the $410,000 to build the Fine Arts Gallery, the Bridges also donated art to the museum. It is now known as the San Diego Museum of Art, and is home to one of the West's finest collections of paintings, sculpture, and other arts; from the old masters to the latest to the modern school.

Cancelled 1942, $3-5

781 AMERICAN LEGION WAR MEMORIAL BUILDING, BALBOA PARK, SAN DIEGO, CALIFORNIA

© H. HERZ   9-2040

Originally called the Home Economy Building, this was the first building to be completed for the Exposition. However, the name and use of the building changed several times. During the Panama–California Exposition household products geared toward housewives were displayed. In 1916, it became the Pan-Pacific building and hosted exhibits from countries along the Pacific Ocean. It was used by the Navy until 1922, when after many renovations, the American Legion took over the building, renaming it the American Legion War Memorial Building. During the California–Pacific International Exposition, it was remodeled to be the Café of the World. With the outbreak of World War II in 1944, the Navy again took control of the building. After the war, the building sat vacant, slowly falling to pieces. In 1963, the building was demolished in order to make way for the Timken Museum of Art.

Circa 1930s, $3-5

81

101A:—The Foreign and Domestic Building, Balboa Park, San Diego, Calif.

During the Panama–California Exposition, the Foreign and Domestic Building hosted exhibits from The Kyosan Kai Company of Japan, which featured chinaware, silk, fabrics, tapestries, and screens. Also presented were a Chinese exhibit of bronzes, silk, a Tea Pavilion and "Streets of Joys." The Streets of Joys allowed visitors to walk down the Ithmus and see women in kimonos and experience Japanese music.

Circa 1915, $3-5

4413. Utah State Building,
Panama-California Exposition, San Diego, 1915.

Utah was one of seven states represented with buildings at the Panama-California Exposition.

Circa 1915, $4-6

EUM, BALBOA PARK, SAN DIEGO, CALIFORNIA—81

From the back: "The Natural History Museum is replete with an interesting collection of fauna, flora, and minerals; also animal life exhibits." The building was designed by William Templeton Johnson, who also did The Fine Arts Gallery.

Circa 1930s, $4-6

4431

AMERICA'S EXPOSITION

California State Building: "High over the main entrance are the historic murals that tell the story of California. The building contains replicas of California's homes and industries, together with displays depicting the triumph of California since the discovery by Cabrillo in the sixteenth century. The sender of this card wrote, "Arrived here yesterday and visited the Exposition. The lighting is beautiful and there is much of interest to see." This visitor was attending The San Diego Century-of-Progress Exposition, 1935-36, held in many new and renovated buildings in Balboa Park.

Cancelled 1935, $3-5

797 ARMORY OF THE 251ST COAST ARTILLERY ANTI-AIRCRAFT, BALBOA PARK, SAN DIEGO, CALIF.

© H. HERZ

9-2056

Also referred to as the California–Pacific Exposition in 1935, California was the only state to have a building. Frescos, designed by Orville Goldner, throughout the building, tell the story of California and illustrate the state's agriculture and industrial growth. The building was requisitioned by the military for World War II and became the Armory of the 21st Coast Artillery Anti-Aircraft Unit.

Circa 1940s, $3-5

CALIFORNIA TOWER, BALBOA PARK, SAN DIEGO, CALIFORNIA—46

From the back: "The California Building, the Tower of which has become symbolic of San Diego, houses an almost priceless collection of ancient American art, architecture and history, and anthropology."

Cancelled 1953, $3-5

The Botanical Building and Landscape

LAGOONS IN FRONT OF BOTANICAL BUILDING.

108A:—Corner of Botanical Bldg. and Portion of Upper Lagoon, Balboa Park, San Diego, Calif.

Landscape architect Kate Session lent her genius to grounds of the Panama Exposition. The lily pond in front of the Botanical Building, originally titled Las Lagunas des Flores (Lakes of Flowers) continues to impress visitors and inspire artists.

Circa 1915, $4-6

When under construction in 1914, the Botanical building was the largest wooden lath structure in the world.

Circa 1915, $3-5

62437

Formal Gardens designed for Balboa Park's first Expo.

Circa 1915, $4-6

The World's Largest Outdoor Organ

LARGEST OUTDOOR ORGAN IN THE WORLD
BALBOA PARK, SAN DIEGO, CALIFORNIA — 1

Largest outdoor organ in the world

From the back: "The Spreckles Memorial organ, the largest outdoor organ in the world, located in Balboa Park, is frequently the scene of public gatherings, pageants, and concerts.

Cancelled 1954, $2-4

An aerial view shows the Open Air Pipe Organ and U.S. Naval Hospital. The Spreckles brothers, John D. and Aldoph, donated this organ for the "people of San Diego," and "the people of the world."

Cancelled 1934, $2-4

4405   OPEN AIR PIPE ORGAN AND U. S. NAVAL HOSPITAL, BALBOA PARK, SAN DIEGO, CALIFORNIA

3A-H1382

Largest Outdoor Pipe Organ in the World,
San Diego, Cal.—1

The sender of this card writes, "Concert is given here every afternoon at three p.m. Where the high school graduation excercises were held last Friday. A beautiful sight indeed, girls wore organdy dresses and hats and every shade imaginable was seen; even white. There were 217 graduates, 91 of which were boys."

Circa 1915, $3-5

The Spreckles Organ had 3400 pipes, with sizes ranging from as small as a pencil to thirty-two feet. A twenty-horse power-blower would pump compressed air into a wind chest, and keys on the console would open valves at the bottom of the pipes. Ernestine Schumann-Heink, a world renowned opera singer and new San Diego resident, performed to a crowd of over 25,000 for the opening of the Panama-California Exposition in 1915. This was the largest audience ever assembled for a musical event in San Diego history and inspired Heink to organize an annual summer festival that would rival any in Europe. However, due to the wars and many unfortunate events, her dream was never realized.

Circa 1915, $5-7

San Diego Zoo

The tallest flight cage in the world presented a spectacular bird display in the Zoological Garden of Balboa Park.

Circa 1915, $4-6

From the back: "The San Diego Zoological Gardens have developed in rank as one of the four largest in America. Here, amid a setting of semitropical gardens, one may find the finest collection in the world, valued at more than one-half million dollars."

Circa 1940s, $3-5

Today, more than 4,000 rare and endangered animals live in the San Diego Zoo. From the back: "The San Diego Zoological Gardens ranks as one of the four largest in America. The Zoo covers an area of over 200 acres amid a setting of semitropical gardens. It contains one of the finest collections in the world. The finest pair of mountain gorillas in captivity are the chief attraction."

Circa 1950s, $4-6

The Plaza de Panama

Plaza de Panama showing U.S. Government and Pan-Pacific buildings for the Panama-California International Exposition.

Circa 1915, $5-7

From the back: "Traversed by the Prado, along which lie Balboa Park's most noteworthy buildings, the Plaza is the center of this world famous Park.. Here, amid the luxuriant foliage of this 1400 acre park, have been held two International Expositions."

Circa 1950s, $5-7

The Cabrillo Bridge was also constructed for the Panama-California International Exposition to extend Laurel Street to the eastern side of Balboa Park and cross the Cabrillo canyon. It is one of the few remaining structures from the exposition still in existence today. The bridge was inspired by a similar bridge in Spain and an aqueduct in Mexico. Frank P. Allen, Panama-California Exposition Director of Works, along with Thomas A. Hunter, an engineer from San Francisco, designed most of the bridge.

Circa 1915, $2-4

Around San Diego

San Diegans are always just a short distance from a beach. The clean air and blue waters of the Pacific pulled people to San Diego as with the tides. Along the long coast, the beaches and surfs vary, creating perfect spots for almost everyone. Mission Beach is the entertainment center, La Jolla is for those who like to be pampered, and Sunset beach is for those who like adventure. The postcards in this chapter show the tranquil beauty and fun spirit of San Diego. At the other end of the spectrum, there are great heights to be achieved around San Diego, with panoramic views that encompass the bay, the Mexican border, and the great city itself.

Highways

From the back: "El Camino Real (The King's Highway), now U.S. Highway 101, follows the coast line for many miles within sight of the rolling waters of the blue Pacific.

Circa 1940s, $2-4

U.S Highway 101 runs north and south along the West Coast, connecting Washington to Southern California.

Circa 1940s, $2-4

680 COAST HIGHWAY, NEAR DEL MAR, LOS ANGELES TO SAN DIEGO, CALIFORNIA

4932-29

Coast Highway near Del Mar Los Angeles to San Diego A main link between Los Angeles and San Diego, Route 101, is simply referred to as 'The 101' by Southern Californians. While The 101 skirts San Diego, some of it can still be found in San Diego County, under a variety of names. As the highway progresses, so do its names. Through the Oceanside neighborhoods, it's The Coast Highway, until Carlsbad. In Del Mar, it's Camino del Mar (Highway of the Sea) and eventually 1-5 near Torrey Pines.

Circa 1920s, $1-3

Travelers could pass from San Diego to neighboring Escondido as early as 1904 on the Poway Grade. Poway is located about thirty miles north and inland from San Diego. An annual bike race is now held along this long road known as the Tour de Poway.

Circa 1910, $1-3

Agriculture

LARGEST POINSETTIA FIELD IN THE WORLD, NEAR SAN DIEGO, CALIFORNIA — 84

From the back: "The poinsettia, known as America's Christmas flower, is in full bloom in San Diego during the Christmas season. Each year the San Diego Heaven on Earth Club makes free public distribution of thousands of poinsettia cuttings." The poinsettia was introduced to California from Mexico by Joel Roberts Poinsett. A large ranch north of San Diego now provides the world with ninety percent of the favorite Christmas flower.

Circa 1920s, $1-3

AVOCADO GROVES, SAN DIEGO, CALIFORNIA—65

From the back: "Truly a treat to the eye are the beautiful evergreen groves of Avocado trees, interset with attractive modern homes and with a background of exceptional natural beauty. The delicious taste and high food value is making this exotic fruit increasingly popular." A native of Mexico, the green fruit was brought to the region by Theosophists, whom came from all over the world to study at the Theosophical Institute in Point Loma. Avocado is a staple ingredient in many southwestern recipes.

Circa 1950s, $2-4

Irrigating an Orange Grove.

"I'll eat oranges for you and you may throw snowballs for me." An obvious taunt from a warm-weathered West Coast resident towards an icy East Coast friend.

Cancelled 1911, $2-4

96

1617. A Field of Calla-Lilies.

San Diego, Cal.

Along with orange groves, farmers and garden enthusiasts on the outskirts of San Diego grew avocados, lemons, figs, pomegranates, and grapes. Here another cash crop— calla lilies.

Cancelled 1910, $2-4

Roping and wrangling, an early card illustrates the cowboy heritage of rural San Diego.

Cancelled 1907, $3-5

Greetings from
SAN DIEGO, CAL.

3721   Branding Cattle Out West

Surf Scene and Point Loma, from Hotel Del Coronado,
Coronado, San Diego, Cal.

Point Loma, a peninsula in the San Diego bay, was discovered by Juan Rodriquez Cabrillo in
the sixteenth century.

Circa 1915, $3-5

Point Loma, San Diego Co., Cal.

The beaches of Point Loma are dotted with rocks and bordered with bluffs. A Victorian gentleman helps his lady cliff hop.

Circa 1910, $2-4

4737. Old Spanish Light House, Point Loma, San Diego, Calif.

The Old Spanish Lighthouse serves as an aid to navigation at Point Loma.

Circa 1920s, $12-14

La Jolla

4598. Seven Caves at La Jolla, San Diego, Cal.

Seven caves are tucked away along the La Jolla Coastline. Only one of the caves is accessible without a canoe or kayak. The waves recede from their watch over these six caves for only about fourteen times a year during low afternoon tides.

Circa 1915, $1-3

'T. CLAUS.' OCEAN BEACH, SAN DIEGO, CAL.

Looking out from the inside of Sunny Jim Cave. This marvel was named by Frank L. Baum, author of The Wizard of Oz and a San Diego resident. Sunny Jim was a cartoon on a cereal box.

Circa 1930s, $1-3

The surf and beaches change each mile along the La Jolla Shore. From the friendly beaches of Kellog Park to Bird Rock, a wonderful place for surfing. These post-cards show a section of the shore that is best left to expert surfers or just to the fish.

Circa 1915, $1-3 each

4617. Breakers five tiers deep. La Jolla, San Diego, Cal.

4611. MAID OF THE MIST, LA JOLLA, SAN DIEGO, CAL.

4626. Watching the Bathers, La Jolla, San Diego, Cal.

The most friendly and picturesque of San Diego beaches is La Jolla Cove. It is one of the most photographed beaches in Southern California.

Circa 1915, $4-6

The spirit of the La Jolla beaches is as free as the surf. Here a view of the bath house and swimming cove, a biplane thrilling the swimmers below.

Circa 1915, $3-5

3863—Bath House and Swimming Cove, La Jolla, San Diego, Cal.

From the back: "Situated one mile north from the community of La Jolla directly on the beach, is the exclusive La Jolla Beach and Tennis Club, Beach Apartments, and Marine Room. Open year round, this beautiful resort affords the visitor ocean and pool bathing, tennis, and pitch and putt golf." The La Jolla Beach and Tennis Club remains a premiere location for visitors. Almost every room has an ocean view.

Circa 1950s, $3-5

LA JOLLA BEACH AND TENNIS CLUB, LA JOLLA, CALIF.—142

4609.   Scene along La Jolla Cliffs, San Diego, Cal.

Framed by cliffs and bluffs, the La Jolla cove offers visitors a beach experience unlike any other.

Circa 1910, $4-6

4614 ALLIGATOR HEAD, LA JOLLA, SAN DIEGO, CALIF.

While this photo shows Alligator Head rock, named for its shape, there is also a Seal Rock along the coast. Message on the back: "I shall miss the sight and sound of the ocean to say nothing of our seals. Did I tell you about the population of seals just off the shore? The story goes the female seals come down to the waters off Southern California for the winter months, returning to Alaska waters in the spring."

Circa 1930s, $1-4

Another view of the Alligator or Sphinx Head rock of La Jolla cove.

Circa 1915, $3-5

4607. Sphinx Head Cave, La Jolla, near San Diego, Cal.

4605. Emerald Cove, La Jolla, San Diego, Cal.

A pleasure craft off the rocky shore of Emerald Cove.

Circa 1915, $2-4

Cathedral Rocks off the coast of La Jolla. From the back: "La Jolla, a charming little town on the coast fourteen miles north of San Diego, California, is famous for its marine gardens and unusual waterfront caves. Fingal's Cave in Scotland is the only other known cave to have the same stratification as La Jolla caves."

Circa 1930s, $3-5

Mission Beach

Mission Beach, California

From the back: "Twenty minutes from San Diego, Mission Beach is a popular resort area. Two miles of excellent sandy bathing beach, amusement center, boating, fishing, aquaplaning, cottages and hotels."

Circa 1950s, $4-6

From the back: "Mission Beach offers an amusement center which consists of surf and bay bathing, boating, camping, fishing, hotels, and swimming pool."

Circa 1940s, $12-14

AMUSEMENT CENTER, MISSION BEACH, SAN DIEGO, CALIF.—145

4825 SUMMER CROWDS AT MISSION BEACH, SAN DIEGO, CALIFORNIA

3A-H1373

Mission Beach has always been popular with the residents and tourists. While the beach attire may have changed, the love of sand, sun and fun remains.

Circa 1930s, $3-5

137A:—The Beautiful Dance Casino, Missio

25099

Mission beach was similar to the action-packed, entertainment-focused East Coast destinations such as Atlantic City, N.J., or Coney Island N.Y.

Cancelled 1926, $4-6

4144. Crawfish Cove, Ocean Beach, San Diego, Cal.

San Diegans enjoy a day on the sand by Ocean Beach at Crawfish Cove. Today, the Ocean Beach community prides itself on its unique old-fashioned spirit.

Circa 1915, $3-5

4712. A SURF SCENE, OCEAN BEACH, SAN DIEGO, CALIF.

Waves crash against the bluffs south of Ocean Beach. The surf along this coastline can be dangerous.

Circa 1920s, $1-3

4705 OCEAN BEACH, SAN DIEGO.

The coves and cliffs of Ocean Beach lie to the south, along Sunset Cliffs.

Circa 1910, $1-3

4721. Natural Bridge, Ocean Beach, San Diego, Cal.

A secluded beach is hidden under this natural bridge.

Circa 1905, $4-6

Sunset Cliffs

This man-made bridge connects two cliffs for visitors enjoying the sunset. The spot attracts surfers, divers, bikers, and gazers alike. However, the conditions can be dangerous and the beaches are unguarded.

Cancelled 1920, $4-6

Visitors have been enjoying gorgeous sunsets and beach for more than a century. It is a popular destination for dreamy beach weddings.

Cancelled 1921, $4-6

72196 SUNSET CLIFFS, SAN DIEGO, CALIFORNIA

Sunset Cliffs is known throughout San Diego as the best place to head to catch spectacular sunsets. Also, the seasonal migration of the California Grey Whales can be seen from the cliffs of Sunset Cliffs as the large mammals make their way to warmer water.

Circa 1920s, $2-4

Coronado

Coronado is a large mass of land connected to the inland by a silver strand of beach and rocks. A thriving community today, the island was once dominated by the Hotel del Coronado and the surrounding Tent City. The name Coronado means "Crowned One." The postcards reflect the area's awesome surf and the amazing hotel. Several movies have been filmed on this fourteen-mile island. A twenty-minute ferry ride makes the island accessible for inlanders and is always a nice outing.

4150. Coronado Islands, Mexico, 17 miles from San Diego, Cal.

The Coronado peninsula juts out into the San Diego Bay, originally connected to the mainland by a silver sand strip and now by the San Diego-Coronado Bridge.

Circa 1910, $1-3

4149. Young Pelicans on Coronado Island, Mexico, 17 miles from San Diego, Cal.

Even the pelicans knew what a great gathering place Coronado was.

Circa 1920, $2-4

4300. Hotel del Coronado, Coronado, San Diego, Cal.

The Hotel del Coronado was built in 1888 by two successful businessmen, Elisha Babcock and H.L. Story. It was billed as one of the largest and most luxurious resorts in the West.

Circa 1915, $3-5

The Hotel del Coronado was nicknamed Lady of the Sea. Among the extravagances of the Hotel del Coronado was the first hotel in the world to have electricity throughout the almost four hundred rooms.

Cancelled 1907, $4-6

Court Hotel del Coronado, San Diego, Cal.

Once compared to The Gardens of Versailles in France, the courtyard of the Hotel del Coronado was breathtaking.

Dated 1905, $3-5

The Hotel's builders, Babcock and Story, ran into financial troubles at the end of the century. John D. Spreckles bought a large share of the hotel and the surrounding land in 1900. While he closed the hotel for renovations, he built Tent City, which brought tourists from all walks of life to Coronado.

Circa 1915, $4-6

BIRD'S EYE VIEW OF CORONADO HOTEL AND TENT SCENE FROM AN AEROPLANE, SAN DIEGO, CAL.

Yachting before Dance Pavilion,
Tent City, Coronado, San Diego, Cal.

The Yacht Club entertained guests with deep-sea fishing, boating, and swimming. On the right,
a dance pavilion offered guests of Tent City nightly entertainment.

Circa 1915, $5-7

TENT CITY, CORONADO, CALIFORNIA.

The Tent City helped make the island the number one attraction and industry in San Diego at
the turn of the century.

Cancelled 1909, $4-6

4299. Hotel del Coronado, Coronado, San Diego, Cal.

"The Lady of the Sea" was the set for several movies, including Some Like It Hot.

Cancelled 1915, $5-7

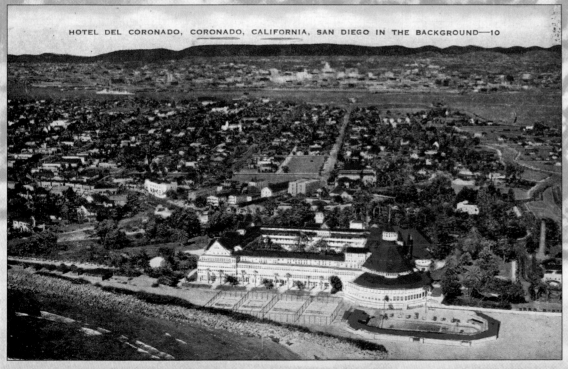

HOTEL DEL CORONADO, CORONADO, CALIFORNIA, SAN DIEGO IN THE BACKGROUND—10

From the back: "For 55 years this internationally famous hotel has been known for its charm, its hospitality, its service, and its beauty. Here are found the Turquoise Pool, the Rainbow Fleet, and a host of other modern facilities for making life more enjoyable."

Cancelled 1950, $3-5

117

850 :—CORONADO ISLAND, SAN DIEGO IN THE BACKGROUND, CALIFORNIA

48743

An aerial overview of Coronado Island.

Circa 1940s, $3-5

Mission Cliffs

For years, Mission Cliffs Garden was a favorite spot for San Diegans. It was the final stop on the trolley line, and therefore easily accessible. The tranquil gardens and breathtaking views were the main attraction, along with the unforgettable ostriches. Many wonderful memories were created here—and then described on postcards sent back home.

Streetcar magnet J.D. Spreckles acquired the park and helped turn it into the lush attraction it became. He was able to use his ownership of the newspaper, The San Diego Union, to encourage people to visit Mission Cliffs, and to collect fares from those who made the journey to the end of his line. However, his attraction dwindled as Balboa Park rose in prominence with the 1915 Expo. Mission Cliffs Gardens closed to the public in 1929. In 1942, the Gardens were sold and sub-divided for residential areas.

A view of the main entrance to Mission Cliffs. Tucked above the Mission Valley in the cliffs, Mission Cliffs Gardens was a popular tourist spot from 1898 to 1942.

Circa 1930s, $2-4

The park was originally owned by the San Diego Electric Railway Company and used an end-of-the-line attraction for riders. The development and maintenance of Mission Cliff Gardens, like so much else in San Diego, can be attributed to J.D. Spreckles. When the San Diego Electric Railway Company went bankrupt in 1892, Spreckles incorporated it to connect his many lines. He also assumed responsibility for the then five-acre garden complex.

Cancelled 1920, $2-4

S.D. 35   MISSION CLIFF GARDENS, SAN DIEGO CALIFORNIA

When Spreckles bought the park, it had only seven palm trees and a pavilion. He hired Scottish gardener John Davidson to develop the area. Davidson devoted himself completely to the project and the gardens grew rapidly.

Circa 1910, $2-4

4513.   Pergola and Pavilion, Mission Cliff Gardens, San Diego, Cal.

Visitors could spend hours picnicking or strolling through the park. Pergolas provided a comfortable space for gazing over the Mission Valley.

Circa 1920s, $2-4

4520. MISSION VALLEY, FROM PERGOLA TERRACE,
MISSION CLIFF GARDENS, SAN DIEGO, CAL.

Views to the west revealed the boundless Pacific Ocean and, to the north, snow capped mountains.

Circa 1920s, $2-4

Bed of Dahlias, Mission Cliff Park, San Diego, Cal.

Concerts and dances were held in this pavilion. However, the construction of Balboa Park for the Panama-California Exposition slowly drew crowds away from Mission Cliffs. This card was made with an Exposition logo on the back, reflecting the park's goal to be part of the 1915 celebration.

Circa 1915, $2-4

Easter Lilies, Mission Cliff Garden, San Diego, Cal.—28

The gardens had plants and flowers from all over the world. A wisteria plant crossed the Pacific three times before arriving in the park. An ostrich farm and aviary were also main attractions. Davidson imported only the best flowers and cared for the gardens until his dying day.

Circa 1920s, $2-4

A miniature Japanese Garden was among the botanical attractions at Mission Cliffs. It was designed by the owner of the similar gardens at the Coronado Hotel in San Diego. Small trees, arched bridges, wisteria flowers, and vine-covered Pergolas made visitors think they had stepped over the Pacific.

Circa 1910, $4-6

4277. Private Japanese Tea Garden, San Diego, Cal.

Beautiful Mission Valley, San Diego Mission in distance, San Diego. Cal.

A view of Mission Valley reveals the rural nature of the setting for the former Mission Cliffs Gardens.

Cancelled 1913, $4-6

124

Sweetwater Dam

The Great
Sweetwater Dam,
San Diego
County, Cal.

The height and structure of this dam made it a tourist attraction when first opened in 1888. Almost three thousand people took part in the National Water Festival in National City in April, 1888 to celebrate the dam.

Cancelled 1907, $2-4

Sweet Water Dam, San Diego, Calif.

When the dam was constructed, it was said to be the highest in the world at ninety feet. It has since been heightened and now stands 127 feet.

Circa 1911, $2-4

Built on a section of the Sweetwater River, where the bed is pinched by rocks then expands into a natural basin, the dam supplies water to the National City area of San Diego. Today almost 177,000 residents rely on the reservoir for their water.

Circa 1920s, $2-4

72195 SWEETWATER DAM, SAN DIEGO, CALIFORNIA

Sweet Water Dam, San Diego, Cal.

The waters raged out of control in 1916 when, after four long years of drought, heavy rains flooded the city. The flood waters washed out another dam, the Lower Otay, killing many people and leaving more homeless. The Sweetwater Dam was also breached. The city of San Diego had employed the services of a rainmaker, Charles Hatfield, to end the drought. He constructed mysterious towers on the Morena Lake that emitted chemicals into the air daily. The city declared the floods 'An act of God' and refused to pay Hatfield.

Circa 1920s, $2-4

93:—Sweetwater Reservoir and Dam, San Diego County, Calif.

During the flood, the waters poured so forcefully over the high wall of the dam, the roaring was said to be heard three miles away. The Sweetwater Dam was one of the first dams to be built in an arch. This design adds strength and is now a standard in dam construction. In 2006, the dam was listed by the American Society of Civil Engineers as a National Historic Landmark.

Circa 1920s, $1-3